DR. KING LIBRARY

New York City

by Joyce Markovics

Consultant: Karla Ruiz, MA
Teachers College, Columbia University
New York, New York

BEARPORT
PUBLISHING

New York, New York

Credits

Cover, © curtis/Shutterstock; TOC Top, © Brooke Becker/Shutterstock; TOC Bottom, © Stuart Monk/Shutterstock; 4–5, © Songquan Deng/Shutterstock and © Luciano Mortula/Shutterstock; 7, © ozgurdonmaz/iStock; 7TR, © ARENA Creative/Shutterstock; 8–9, © Christian Mueller/Shutterstock; 10–11, © Kotsovolos Panagiotis/Shutterstock; 12, © rorem/Shutterstock; 12–13, © littleny/Shutterstock; 13, © The Stapleton Collection/Bridgeman Images; 14, © Kusska/Shutterstock; 15, © Marco Rubino/Shutterstock; 16, © spyarm/Shutterstock; 17, © Black Star/Alamy Stock Photo; 18, © Robyn Mackenzie/Shutterstock; 19 (T to B), © Valentina Razumova/Shutterstock, © Stockagogo, © Craig Barhorst/Shutterstock, and © AlessandroBiascioli/Shutterstock; 20–21, © AndreyKrav/iStock; 22 (Clockwise from Top Right), © T photography/Shutterstock, © TTstudio/Shutterstock, © meunierd/Shutterstock, © Matej Hudovernik/Shutterstock, and © Marco Rubino/Shutterstock; 23 (T to B), © anyaivanova/Shutterstock, © Robyn Mackenzie/Shutterstock, © rorem/Shutterstock, and © oneinchpunch/Shutterstock; 24, © UTBP/Shutterstock.

Publisher: Kenn Goin
Senior Editor: Joyce Tavolacci
Creative Director: Spencer Brinker
Photo Researcher: Thomas Persano

20453634

Library of Congress Cataloging-in-Publication Data

Names: Markovics, Joyce L., author.
Title: New York City / by Joyce Markovics.
Description: New York, New York : Bearport Publishing, 2018. | Series: Citified! | Includes bibliographical references and index.
Identifiers: LCCN 2017005152 (print) | LCCN 2017007382 (ebook) | ISBN 9781684022304 (library bound) | ISBN 9781684022847 (Ebook)
Subjects: LCSH: New York (N.Y.)—Juvenile literature.
Classification: LCC F128.33 .M36 2018 (print) | LCC F128.33 (ebook) | DDC 974.7/1—dc23
LC record available at https://lccn.loc.gov/2017005152

For more information, write to Bearport Publishing Company, Inc., 45 West 21st Street, Suite 3B, New York, New York 10010. Printed in the United States of America.

10 9 8 7 6 5 4 3 2 1

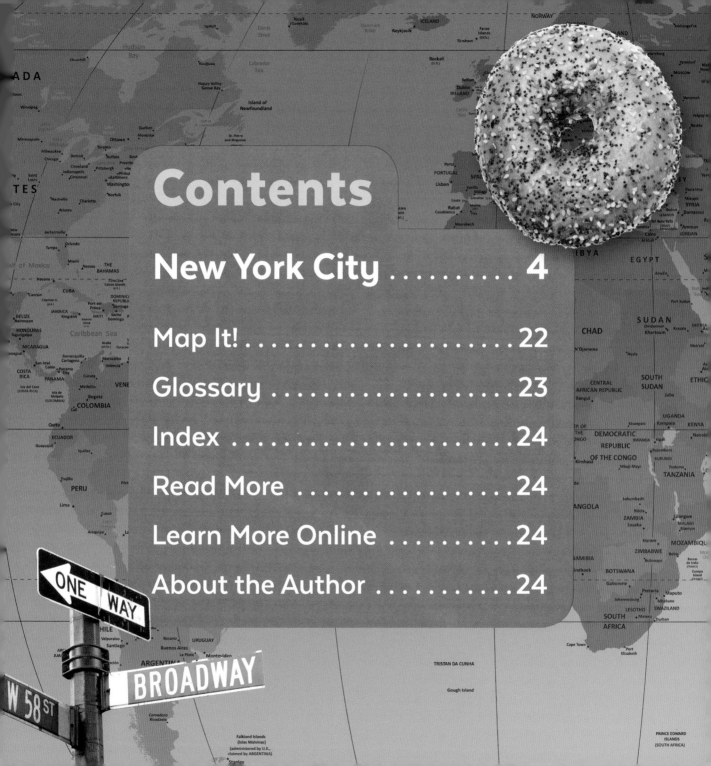

Contents

Welcome to NEW YORK CITY

The City That Never Sleeps!

New York City is also called the Big Apple.

New York City is the biggest city in the United States!

More than 8 million people live there.

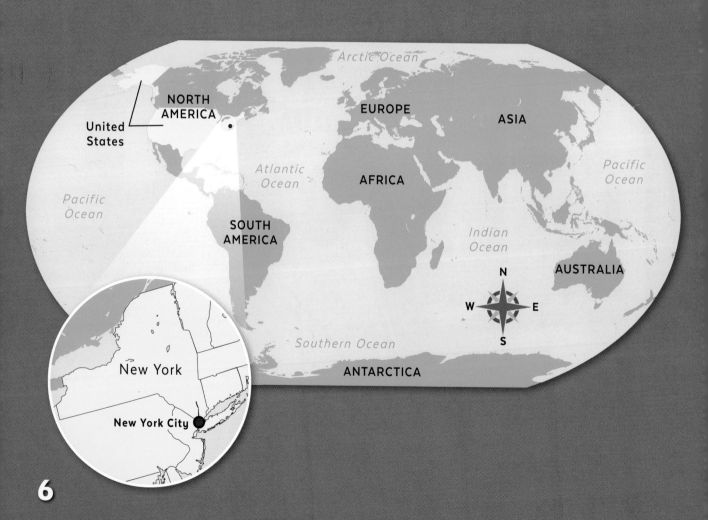

Around 800 different languages are spoken in New York City, or NYC.

New York City has five boroughs, or sections.

They are Manhattan, Brooklyn, Queens, the Bronx, and Staten Island.

Brooklyn is home to Coney Island. It's one of the oldest amusement parks in the country!

9

Manhattan is known for its super tall buildings.

In fact, the word *skyscraper* was **invented** in New York City!

NYC's tallest building is One World Trade Center. It rises 1,776 feet (541 m).

One World
Trade Center

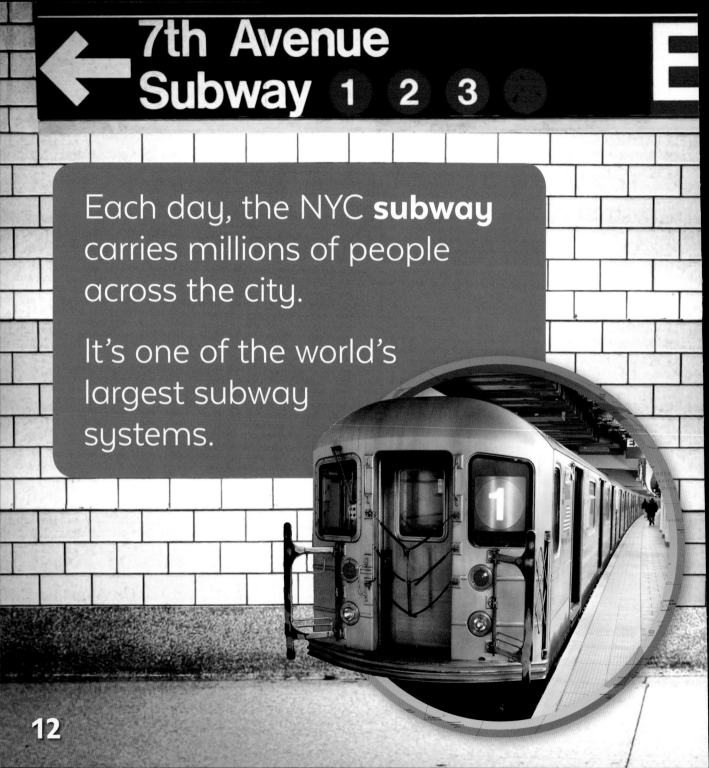

7th Avenue
Subway 1 2 3

E

Each day, the NYC **subway** carries millions of people across the city.

It's one of the world's largest subway systems.

Laid end to end, the subway's tracks would stretch all the way to Chicago!

The NYC subway system is more than 100 years old.

Take a stroll in a New York City park.

There are more than 1,700 of them!

Central Park is the most visited park in the country. About 25 million people go there each year.

One of the most striking parks is the High Line.

It was built above the street on an old railroad track.

The Statue of Liberty looks out over NYC.

She stands more than 305 feet (93 m) tall.

The statue was a gift from France in 1885.

Visitors have to climb 354 steps to reach her crown!

What else is famous about the city?

Its food!

Bite into a giant **pastrami** sandwich.

Grab a sizzling hotdog—or a huge, salty pretzel.

New Yorkers love pizza. There are more than 1,000 pizzerias in the city!

More than 50 million **tourists** visit NYC each year.

Come see why so many people love the city!

People enjoy visiting NYC's busy Times Square.

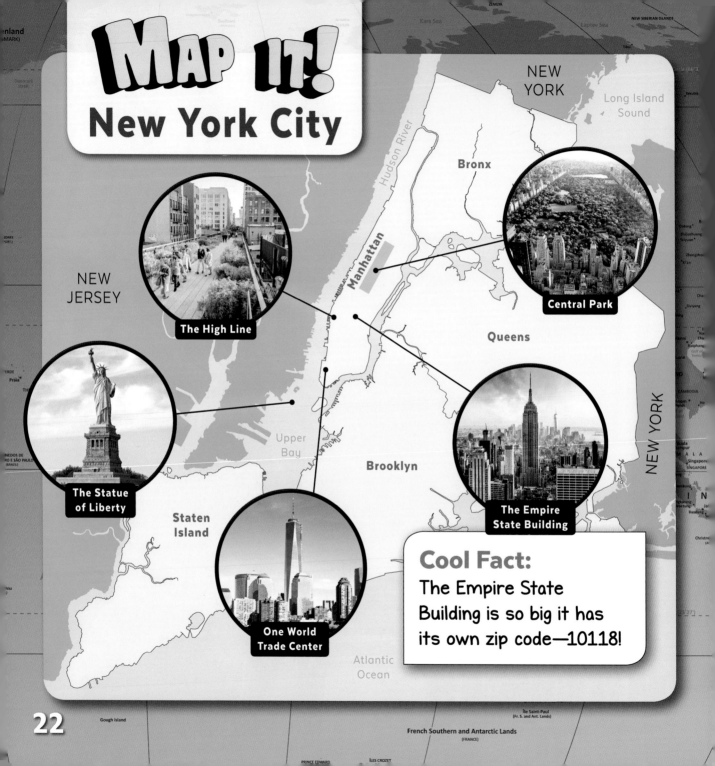

MAP IT!
New York City

NEW YORK

Long Island Sound

Bronx

Hudson River

NEW JERSEY

Manhattan

The High Line

Central Park

Queens

The Statue of Liberty

Upper Bay

Brooklyn

The Empire State Building

Staten Island

One World Trade Center

Atlantic Ocean

NEW YORK

Cool Fact:
The Empire State Building is so big it has its own zip code—10118!

invented (in-VEN-tuhd) first created

pastrami (*puh*-STRAH-mee) seasoned smoked beef, served in thin slices

subway (SUHB-*way*) an electric train that runs underground

tourists (TOOR-ists) people who travel to and visit places for pleasure

Index

Read More

Hannigan, Paula. *New York City.* Riverside, NJ: Accord Publishing (2012).

Melmed, Laura Krauss. *New York, New York! The Big Apple from A to Z.* New York: HarperCollins (2005).

Learn More Online

To learn more about New York City, visit
www.bearportpublishing.com/Citified

About the Author

Joyce Markovics lives and works in New York. Her favorite thing to do in New York City is visit the Metropolitan Museum of Art.